B!LMEM

ZDOKUZ VARIATIONS

ABDULLAH ENISSA VAS

Abdullah Enis Savas
is a poet, writer, and translator born in Vienna, Austria. He earned his BA in American Studies at Istanbul University. He published his debut poetry collection in 2022: What God Meant by Flowers (Ebabil Publishing). He has published a short-story collection: Don't Wait For Me (Pruva Publishing, 2021), and an interdisciplinary work: Kalemler (Fabrik, 2023).

@aenissavas
enissavash@hotmail.com

All rights reserved.
Copyright © 2023 by Abdullah Enis Savas
ISTANBUL

B!LMEM

intro

The works in this book were created by transforming the covers of BUZDOKUZ. The numbers in the titles of the works indicate which issue of the magazine's cover was used. Bonuses are extras independent of covers. Hakan Şarkdemir is the terminator in Bonus I. We would like to thank BUZDOKUZ, paper view books, the owners of the original images on the covers of the magazine and the words we quoted in the work, and everyone who was involved and helped in some way.

B!LMEM

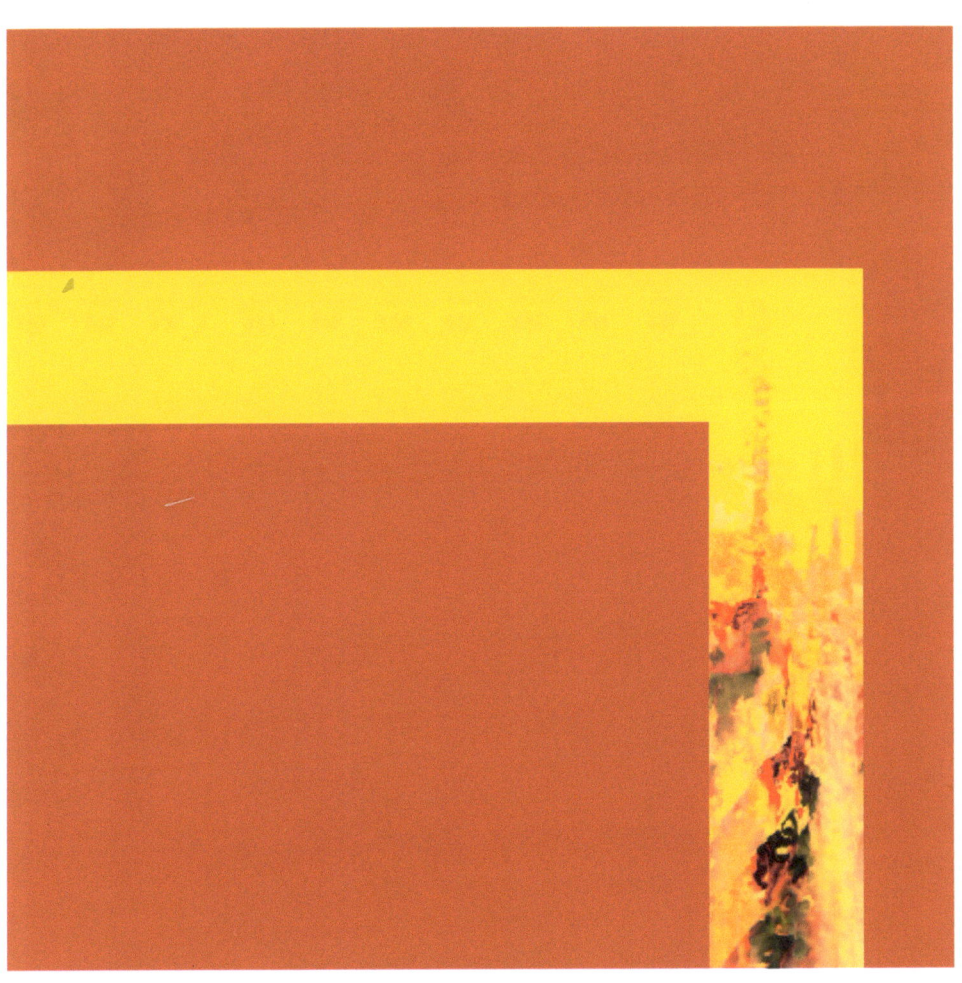

no. 1
introduction: disappearing acts [strictly 9's and MAC's]

no. 2
rast and the boşluk

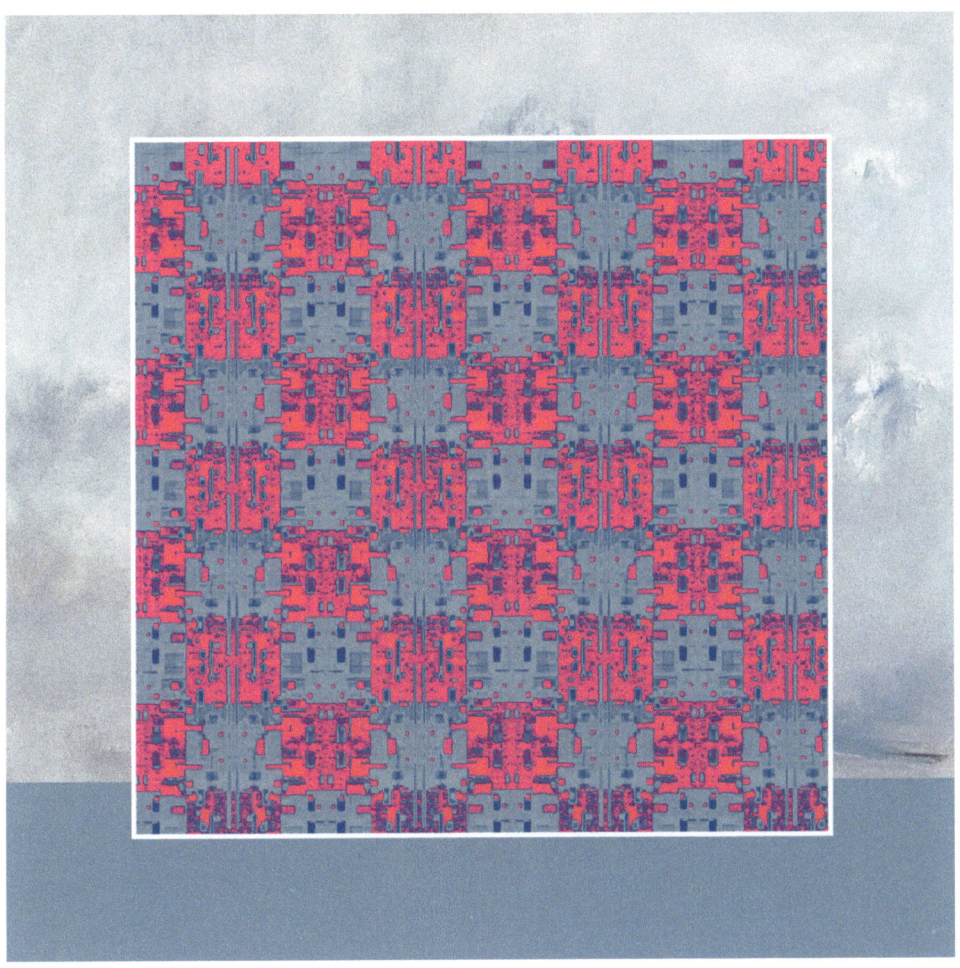

no. 3
die winterreise

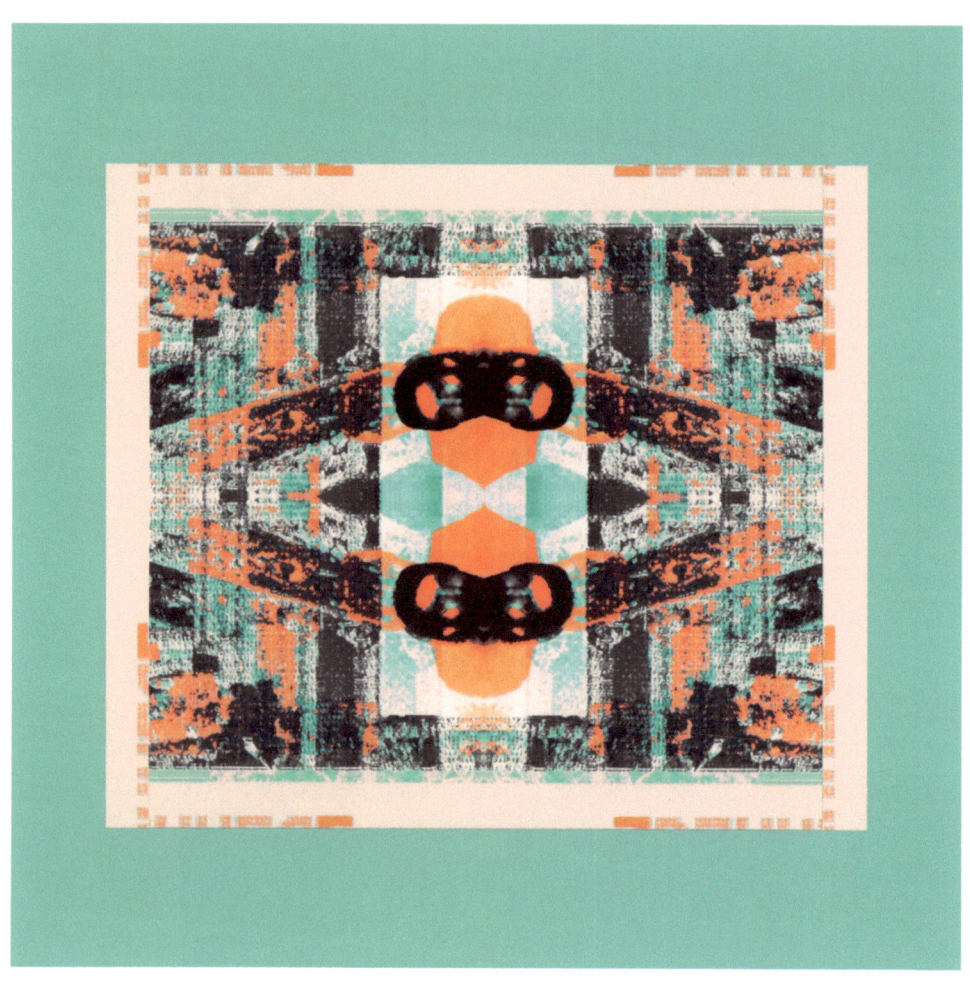

**no. 4
zarifoğlu effect**

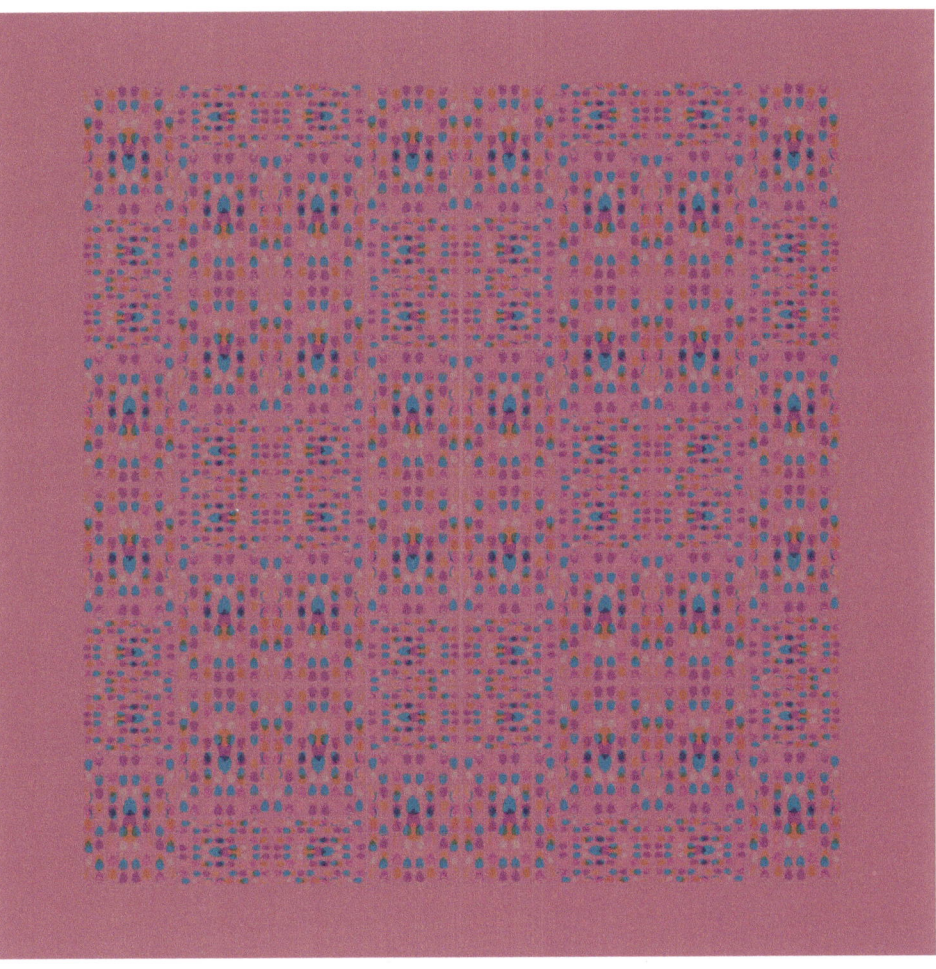

no. 5
al-andalusi candy

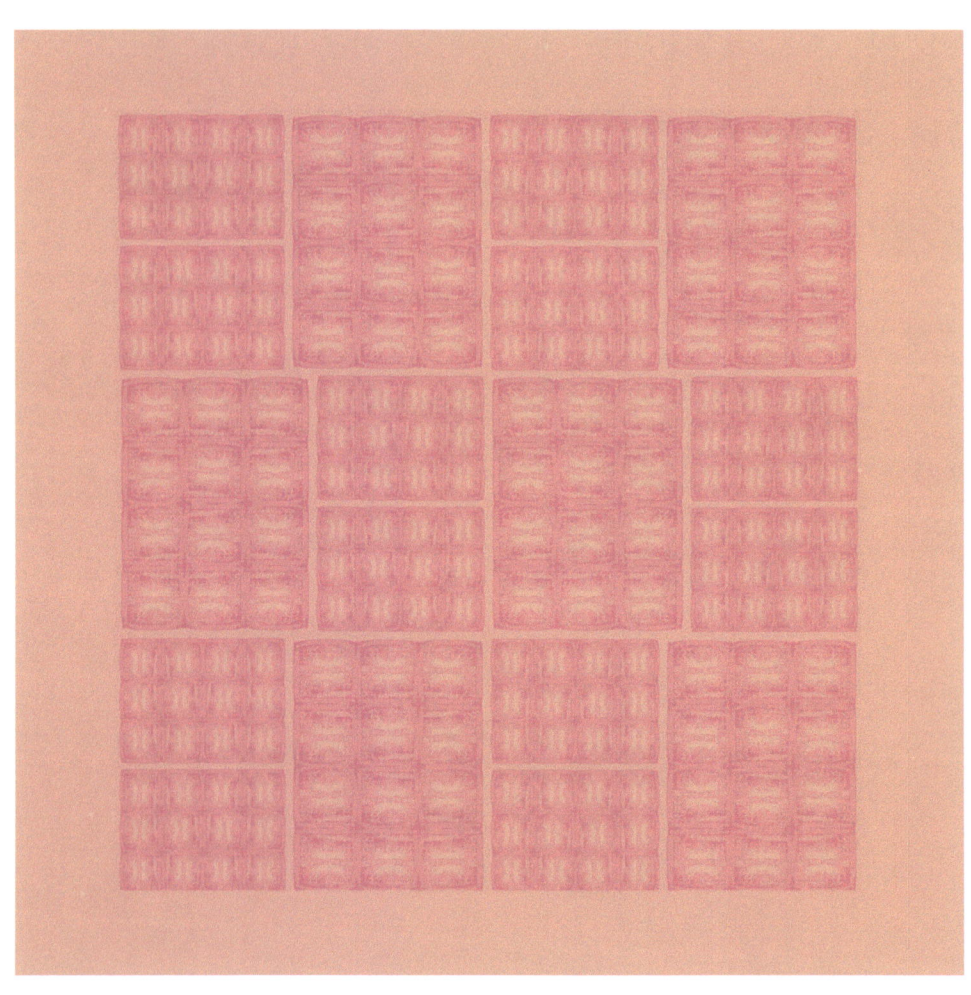

no. 6
ibn-i arabî [strawberry flavored]

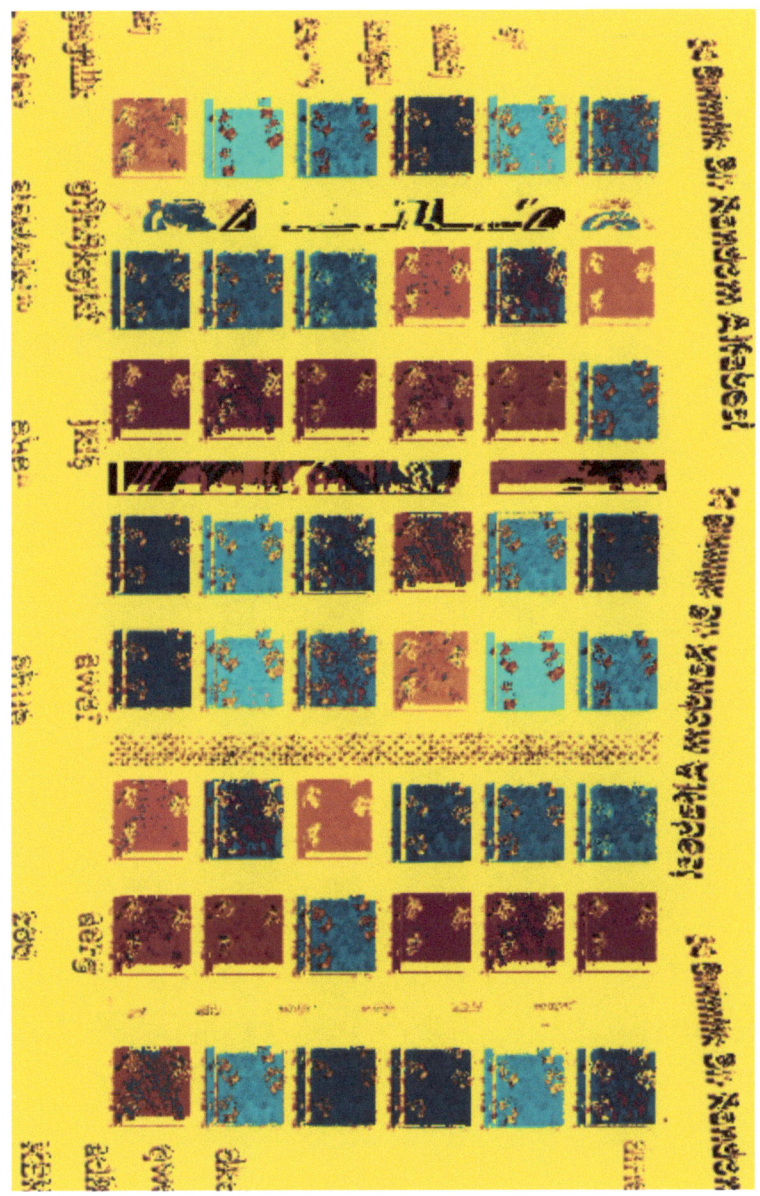

no. 7
ünal und ahahaha

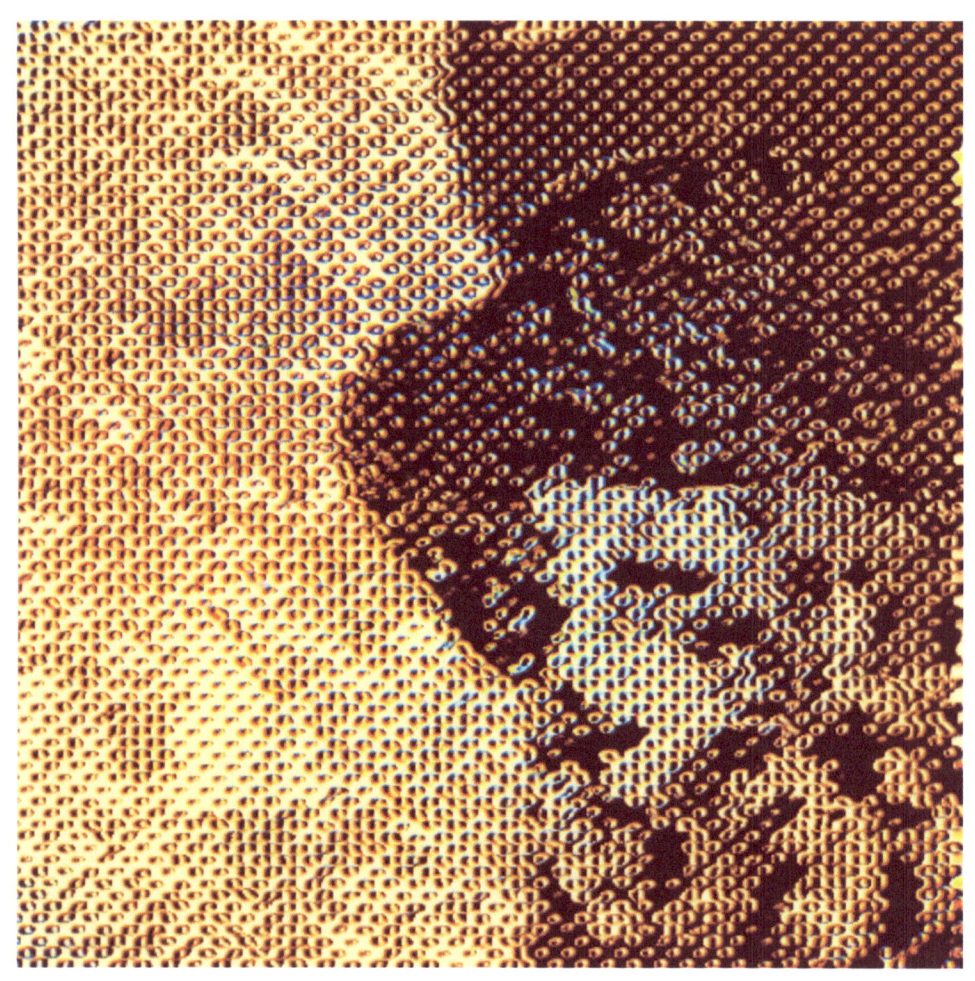

no. 8
mozart the mack [1970 somethin']

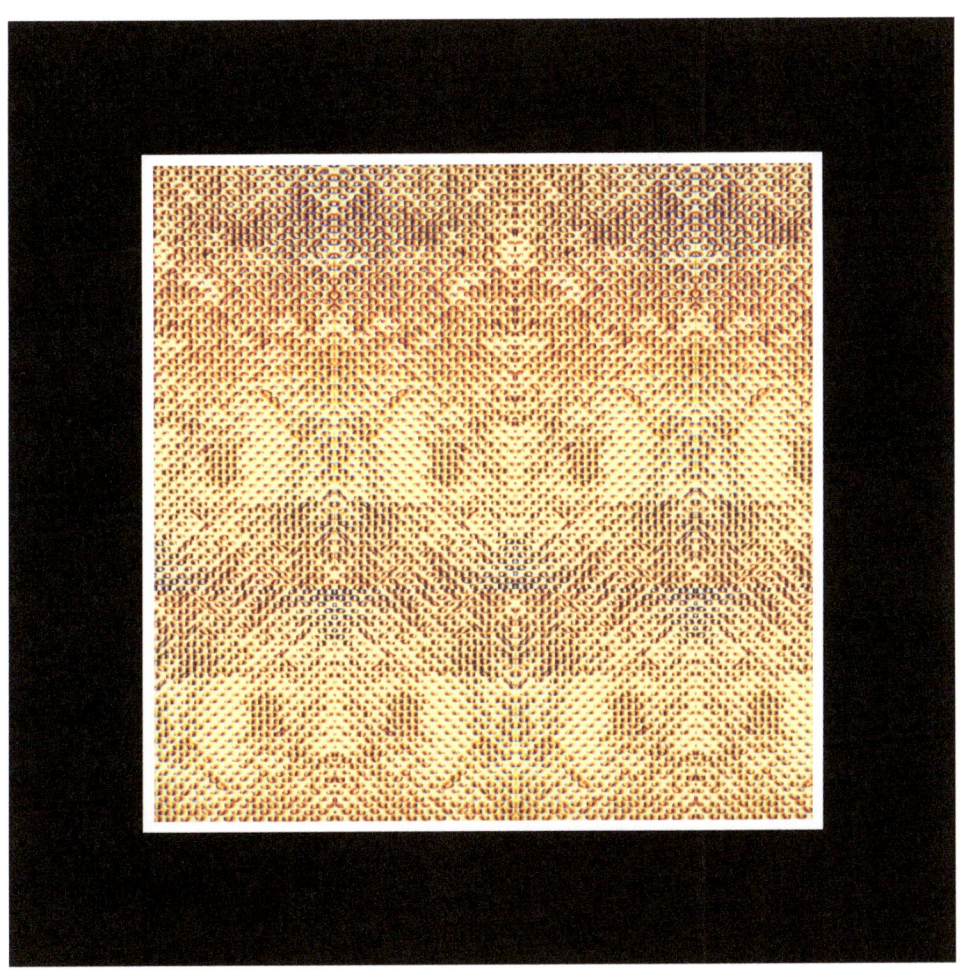

no. 8
interlude I: freaky [rüküşlük estetiği]

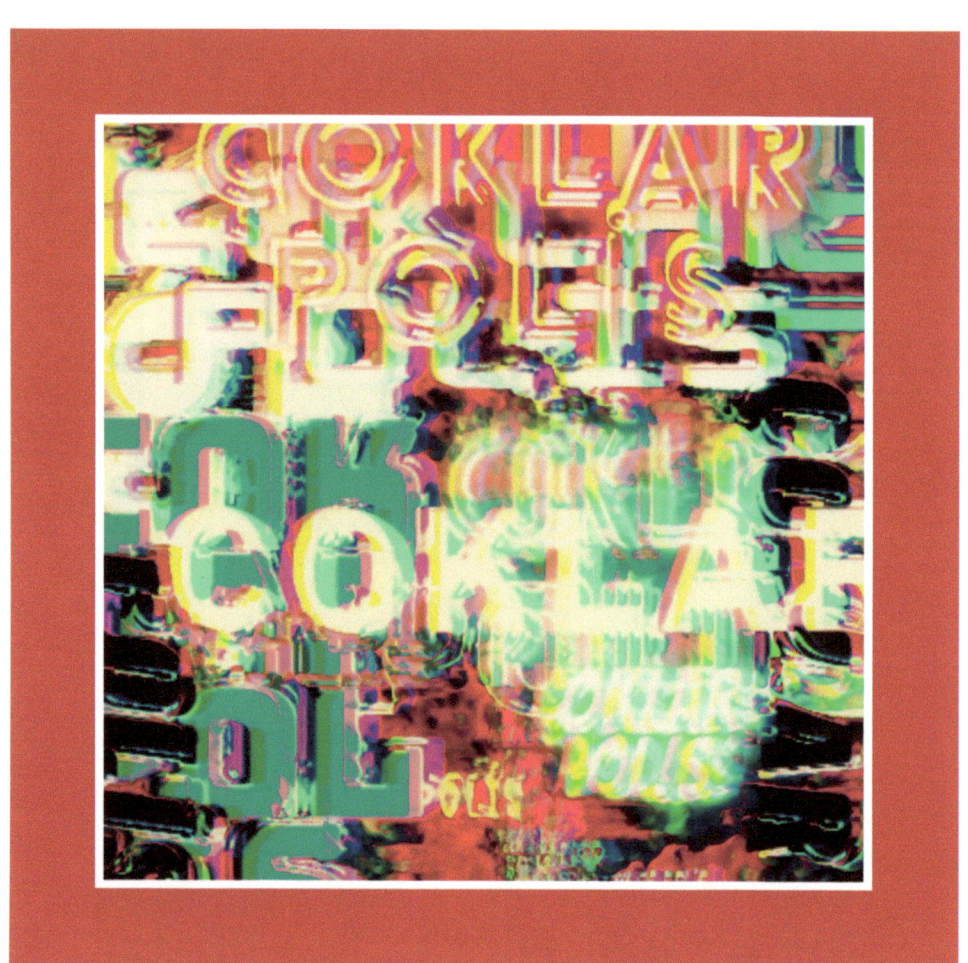

no. 9
fist of özbahçe

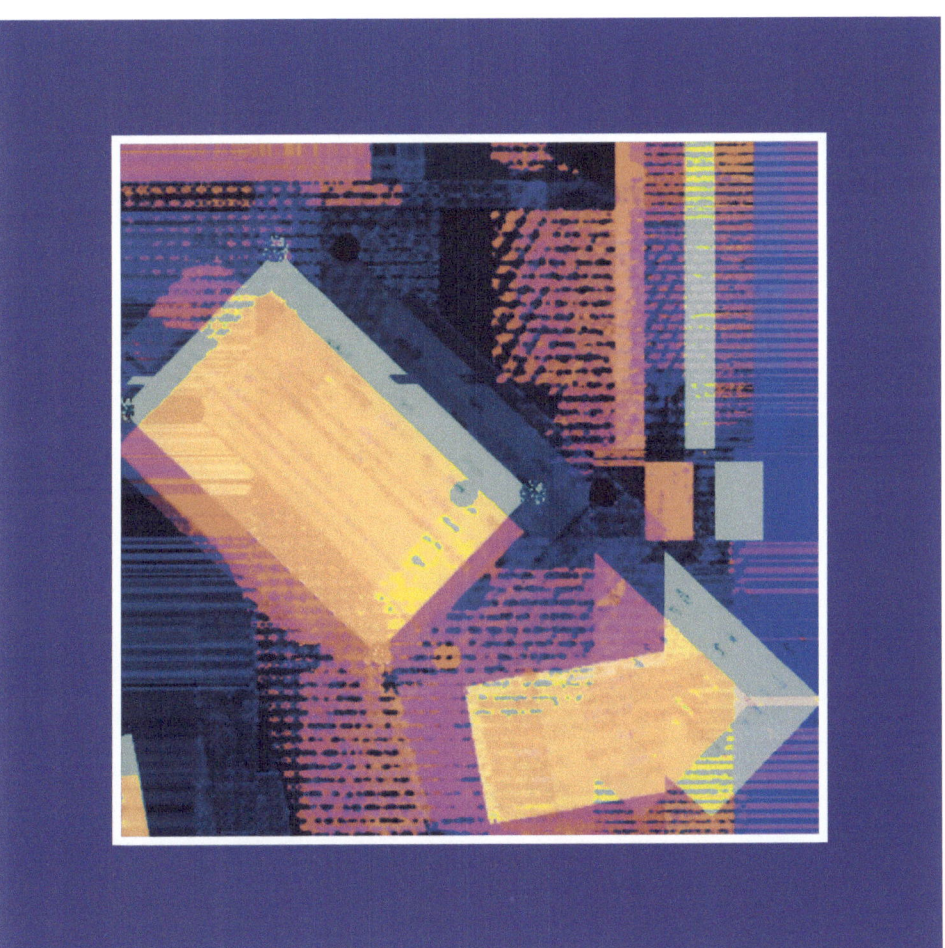

no. 10
90s smile

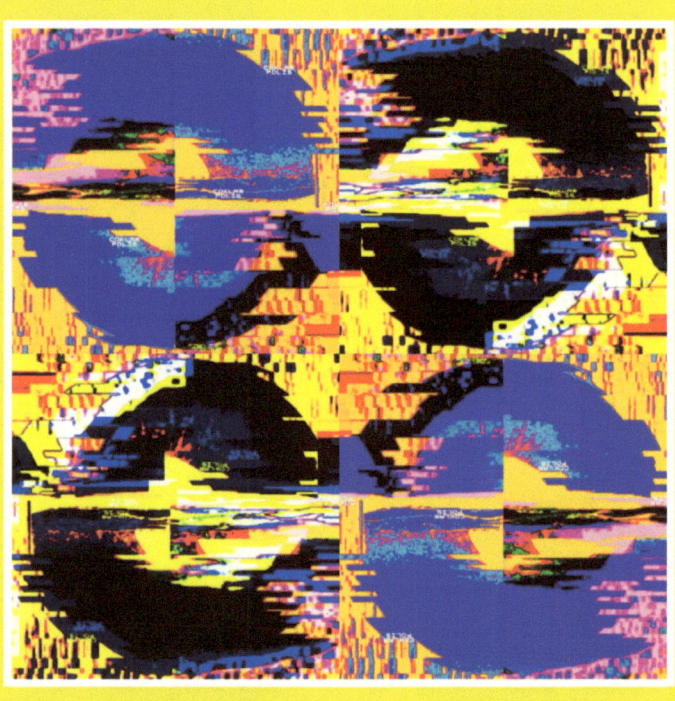

no. 11
çoklar polis

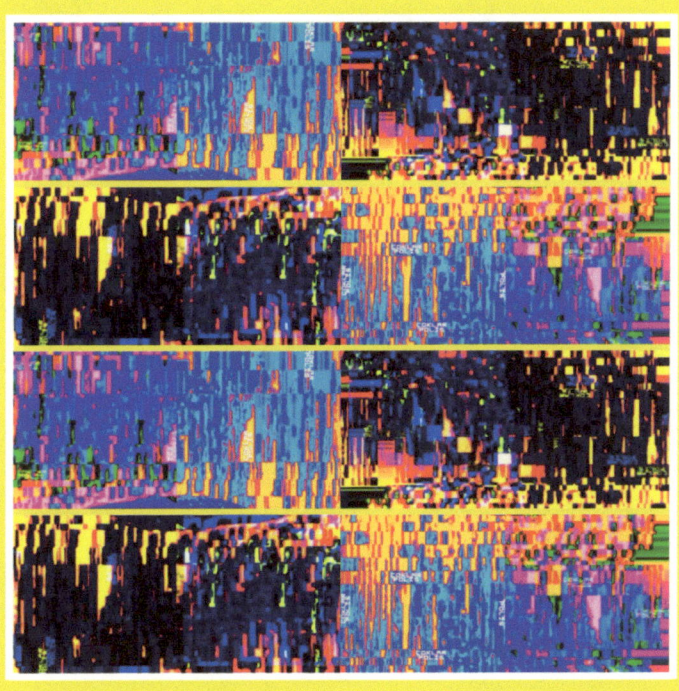

no. 11
interlude II: dewdropper

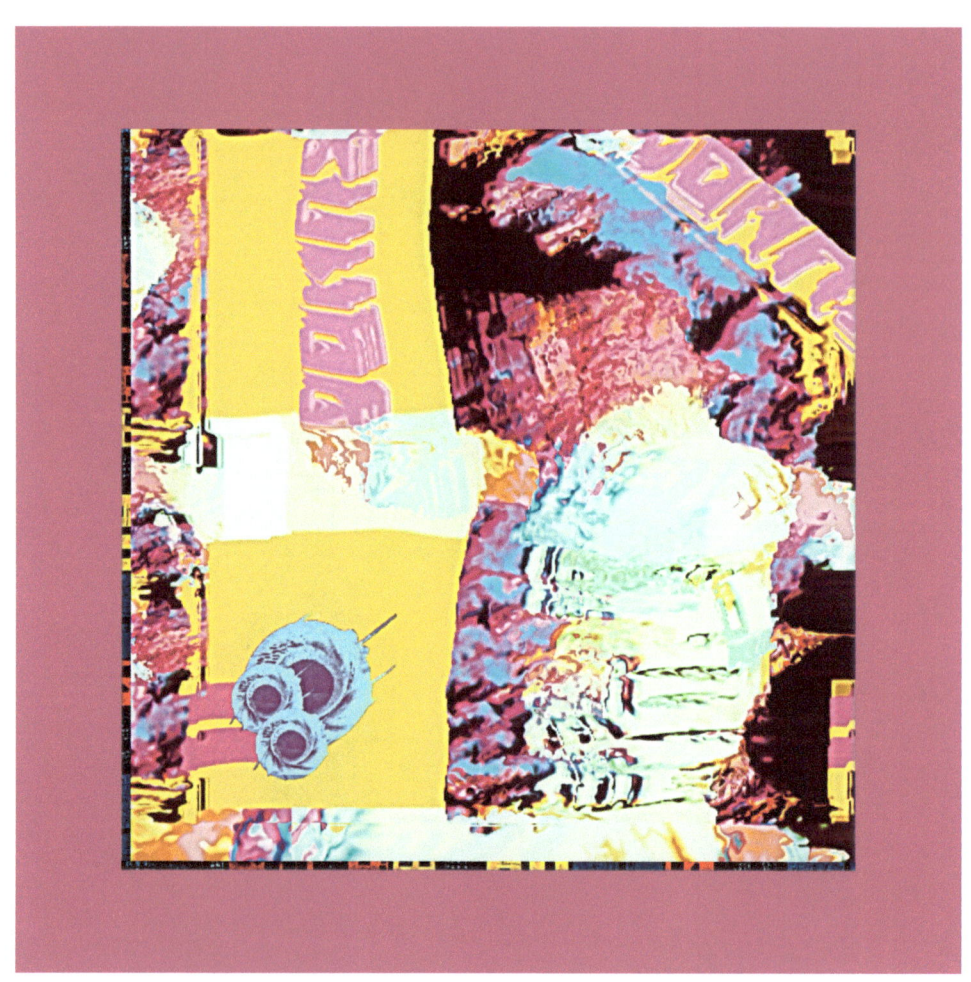

no. 12
zip-n-check

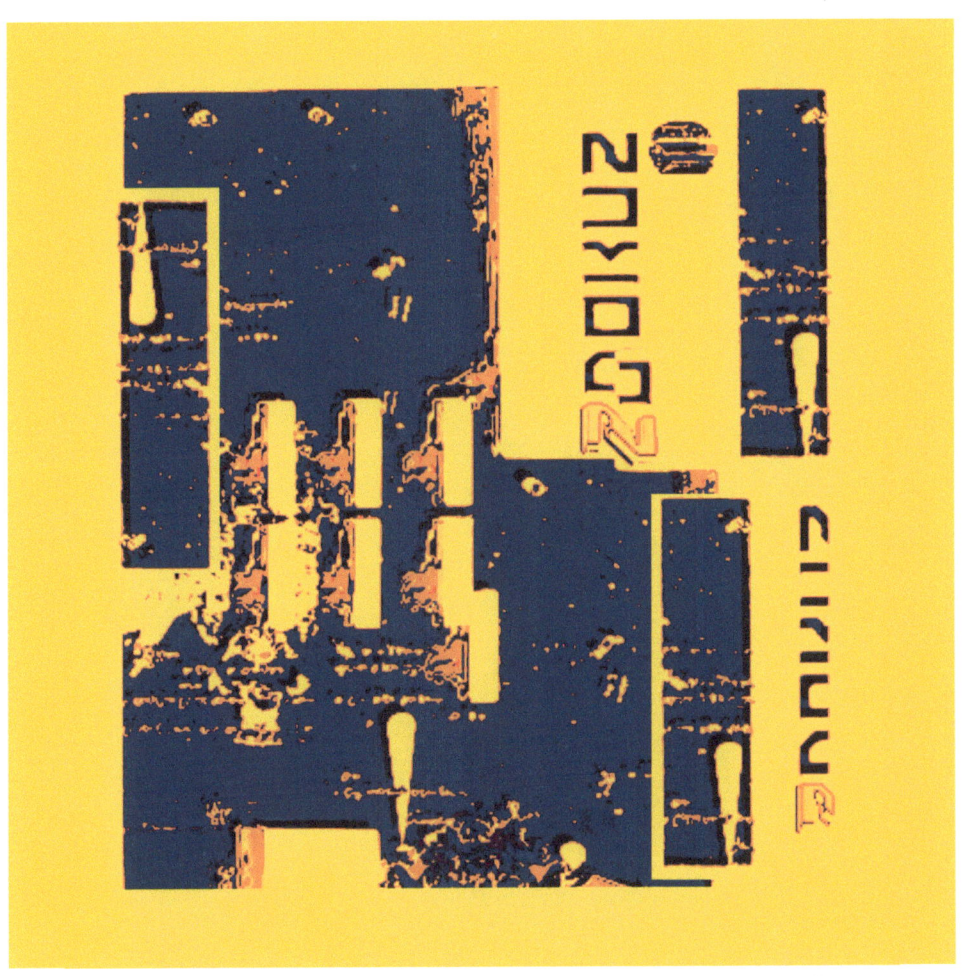

no. 13
coda: electro-poetz

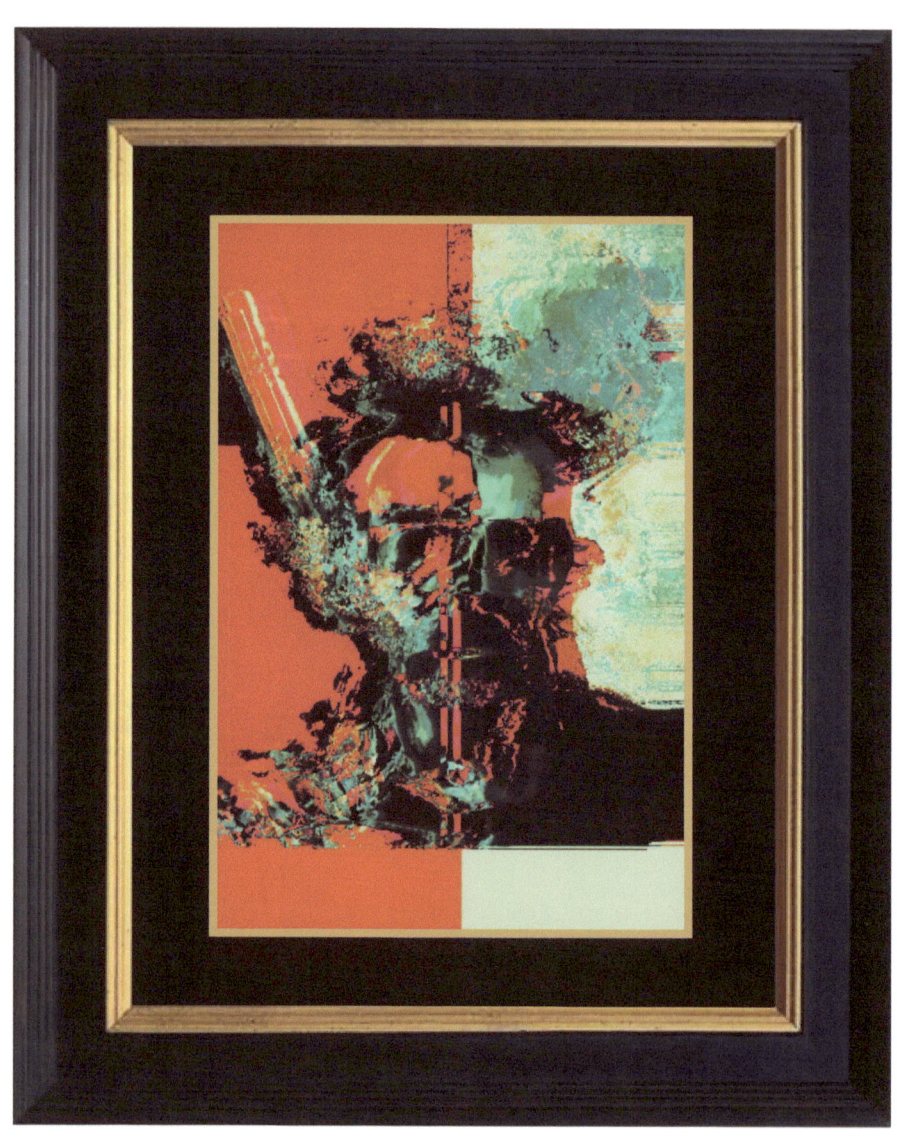

bonus I
a portrait of the artist as a terminator

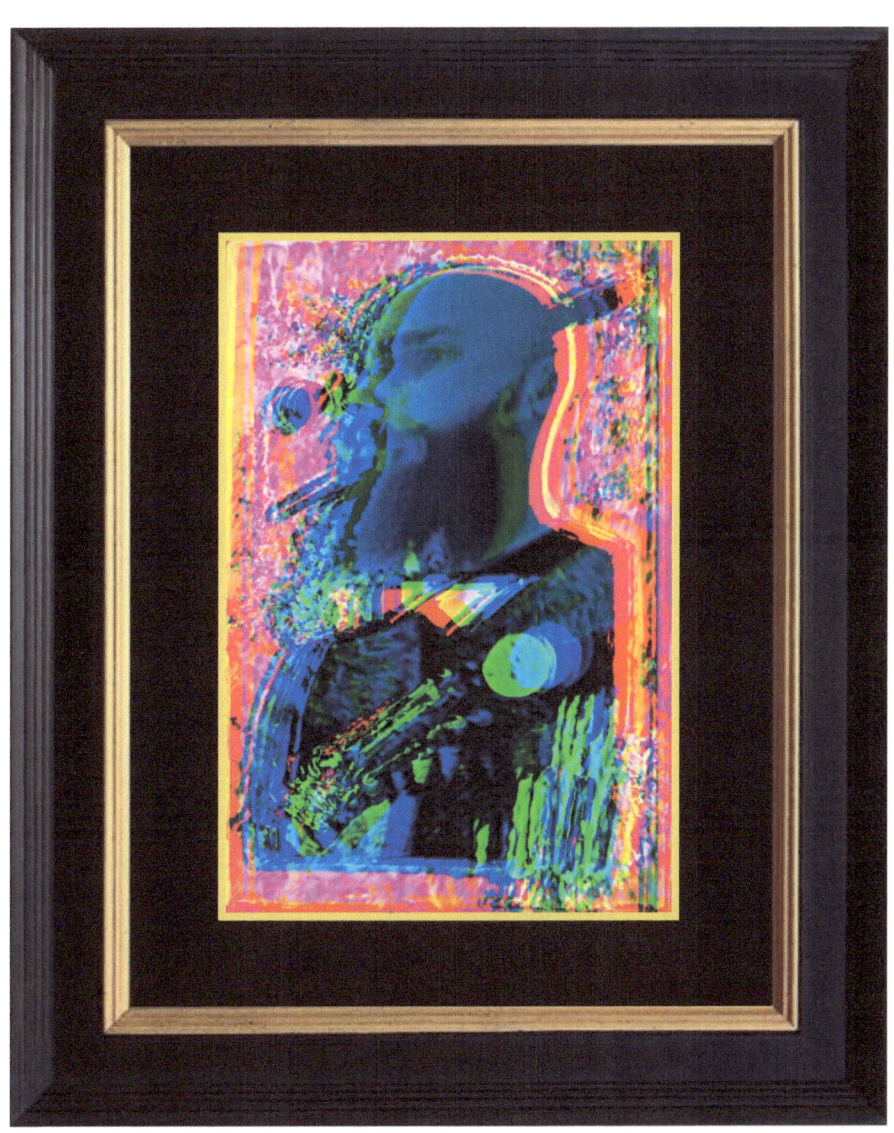

bonus II
self-portrait: the general

B!LMEM

www.ingramcontent.com/pod-product-compliance
Lightning Source LLC
Chambersburg PA
CBHW040352220526
45473CB00009B/2861